WARRIOR'S WITNESS

Autobiography of Army Soldier
Albert Lifschultz

WARRIOR'S WITNESS

Autobiography of Army Soldier
Albert Lifschultz

Edited by Vera Marie Verna

LEONINE PUBLISHERS
PHOENIX, ARIZONA

Published by

Leonine Publishers LLC
Phoenix, Arizona, USA

ISBN-13: 978-1-942190-60-8
Library of Congress Control Number: 2020909788
10 9 8 7 6 5 4 3 2 1

Visit us online at www.leoninepublishers.com
For more information: info@leoninepublishers.com

Dedicated to my little daughter
Rosegale Lifschultz
12/19/1965 – 3/30/1970

&

She left for heaven at age four,
inspiring me with profound words of
healing on her death bed.

Contents

Foreword

Albert Lifschultz, a decorated and honored veteran of three wars, is a witness to the inherent sanctity of life. As a young, 17-year-old soldier, he was on his way to Bastogne to support the Battle of the Bulge during World War II.

After he successfully parachuted with his company, he stepped on a land mine while on the march to Bastogne. Wounded, blinded, and bleeding out, he had an out-of-body experience. He was discovered by a German company on their way to Bastogne as well, bayonetting all prisoners, especially those mortally wounded.

Looking at his papers and his name, Lifschultz, the German's mistook it for an old German royal name and the name's reputation for royal brave warriors.

Just as they were about to bayonet Albert, an officer interrupted. Instead, they took him by ambulance to a German hospital in Heidelberg, where they restored his sight, and saved his life after several operations. All the while they thought he was of German royal stock, not knowing he was a German Orthodox Jew.

This young Army soldier survived sexual abuse as a child, suffered the early deaths of his wife and young daughter and later his young son. He survived POW camp during World War II. He went on to fly 50 sorties in the Korean war, and survived from the wounds he received there. He also miraculously survived a helicopter crash while flying in Viet Nam to bring food to the troops on Christmas Day.

This is a true story about a man and His God. Albert was able to survive atrocious mental and physical wounds by trusting in His Lord to protect him all the days of his life. He extends an invitation to others who have also been mortally wounded mentally, or physically from abuse, or have experienced war, to read his story in hopes that they can find healing as well.

CHAPTER 1

Farewell Party/Off to War

Yes, we are all here, March 8, 1944. Mom and Dad, the rabbi, and about 150 family and friends wish me well with a grand send-off to what they think is to the new military officer training program!

I studied very hard at Newark Central High School in order to apply and to be accepted into the new AS/VS military program for officer training (Army/Navy), a new military program, precursor of the now ROTC. My parents were proud that I was allowed to graduate at age 17 and accepted to enter officer training and to finish there with college.

The farewell party was planned for March 8, today!

Just one week before the program was to begin, it was cancelled due to the war's need of every military man. I did not tell my family that the program was cancelled and I was not headed for Michigan. In fact, I had volunteered with the Army, since I was already enlisted through the cancelled program. I was on my way to war. I was headed to Fort Dix and off to World War II.

My father, Gustave Lifschultz, came to this country from Frankfurt, Germany, when he was eight years old. The "Junkers of Germany" were 99 families from antiquity who ruled Germany. "Von Lifschultz" was a royal name. Their servants took the royal name Lifschultz as did my Jewish father's family.

My German Orthodox Jewish father would find out later—in just six months—that the "Lifschultz" name would save the life of his son near the Battle of the Bulge.

Gustave and his wife Rose Michaels were very successful. They owned a hotel and several rental properties in Irvington, New Jersey, but later were forced to relocate to Newark, New Jersey, due to a large population of German Americans who were pro-Nazi. My Jewish brothers were bullied and mistreated on a daily basis.

Finally, the family moved to Newark where they opened the Clinton Manor Catering Company in 1932. The business grew quickly and became well known in the area for kosher catering, hosting major events at the site.

Located in downtown Newark at 104 Clinton Avenue, it became a landmark. The largest kosher catering company in New Jersey.

Albert Lifschultz, age 17,
Clinton Manor, Newark, New Jersey.

Today, my grand send-off is at Clinton
Manor with the rabbi giving the blessing.
Family and friends were excited for me
going off to what they thought was officer
training school and college.

I am the youngest of the three boys.
My brother Herbert and his wife are here,
but brother Murray had joined the Army
as a combat medic and was recovering
from surface wounds at an Army hospital.

Just before the party, I said goodbye to my high school sweet heart, Delores Goldberg. I liked her a lot. She was so cute with her turned up nose, and very intelligent. She looked like the actress, Yvonne DeCarlo, of the 1940s. She cried and asked me to write to her. She was very patriotic and proud of me. I did write and kept in touch, but after the war I was told that she was engaged to be married. I was okay with that. People change and I certainly was to change as a result of the events to come.

March 9, 1944, finally on my way. My father drove me to Newark National Guard Induction Center where I would then leave for Fort Dix for shots, a physical, and given my full uniform. I was assigned to do basic training at Camp Wheeler, Macon, Georgia. I know a lot of recruits here from Newark Central High School. I weighed in at 230 pounds, 6 feet tall. I was known at my school to be very aggressive and tough.

I did not hesitate to fight whomever, for whatever reason, and my size and attitude served me well, especially with football and wrestling.

My school mate, Al DeRogatis, who played some serious football with me in high school, became All American at Duke University and later played football with the New York Giants. Yes, I thrived on "the combat mode" for football and wrestling.

My early passion was music. Classical music. Who could imagine that I would later sing at the Met in New York and marry an opera singer who was to sing at the Met with me.

It was in elementary school when I became involved for years with local music camps. I was also singing in the choir at a Catholic church, and it was there that I was sexually abused by a Catholic priest who was the choir master.

I tried to stuff it and didn't tell anyone. My trusting parents had no idea why I was vomiting in the mornings before choir practice. My smoldering anger and disgust over this injustice built up quickly and deeply.

By high school, I was a very angry young man. I owned a fast motorcycle that my parents did not know about, and I was racing fast cars as well. I hoped I would die in a car crash.

I had no desire to live with this secret any longer. I had hoped to become an architect or engineer, but when the officer's training program was offered, I quickly enlisted and was accepted.

I wanted to distance myself from home, as if it would help the nagging pain. I did not tell my parents that the program was cancelled. I wanted to go to war instead. Eager to do some serious damage to the Nazis who were harming and abusing people.

As an Orthodox Jew, I was brought up reading the Psalms. I prayed my favorite Psalms 91 and 23 every day.

In boot camp, I was given a Jewish pocket Bible issued to us by President Franklin Roosevelt. I treasured it and prayed every night with it.

I prayed in the field under a blanket with a flash light, wherever and whenever I could. I never missed a day—basic training camp, POW camp, hospitals, all three wars. I carried it in my uniform pocket over my heart. I trusted that my Lord would help me as He promised in the Psalms.

Psalm 23, King James Version (KJV)

The LORD is my shepherd; I shall not want.

2 He maketh me to lie down in green pastures: he leadeth me beside the still waters.

3 He restoreth my soul: he leadeth me in the paths of righteousness for his name's sake.

4 Yea, though I walk through the valley of the shadow of death, I will fear no evil: for thou art with me; thy rod and thy staff they comfort me.

5 Thou preparest a table before me in the presence of mine enemies: thou anointest my head with oil; my cup runneth over.

6 Surely goodness and mercy shall follow me all the days of my life: and I will dwell in the house of the LORD for ever.

Psalm 91, King James Version (KJV)

He that dwelleth in the secret place of the most High shall abide under the shadow of the Almighty.

2 I will say of the LORD, He is my refuge and my fortress: my God; in him will I trust.

3 Surely he shall deliver thee from the snare of the fowler, and from the noisome pestilence.

4 He shall cover thee with his feathers, and under his wings shalt thou trust: his truth shall be thy shield and buckler.

5 Thou shalt not be afraid for the terror by night; nor for the arrow that flieth by day;

6 Nor for the pestilence that walketh in darkness; nor for the destruction that wasteth at noonday.

7 A thousand shall fall at thy side, and ten thousand at thy right hand; but it shall not come nigh thee.

8 Only with thine eyes shalt thou behold and see the reward of the wicked.

9 Because thou hast made the LORD, which is my refuge, even the most High, thy habitation;

10 There shall no evil befall thee, neither shall any plague come nigh thy dwelling.

11 For he shall give his angels charge over thee, to keep thee in all thy ways.

12 They shall bear thee up in their hands, lest thou dash thy foot against a stone.

13 Thou shalt tread upon the lion and adder: the young lion and the dragon shalt thou trample under feet.

14 Because he hath set his love upon me, therefore will I deliver him: I will set him on high, because he hath known my name.

15 He shall call upon me, and I will answer him: I will be with him in trouble; I will deliver him, and honour him.

16 With long life will I satisfy him, and shew him my salvation.

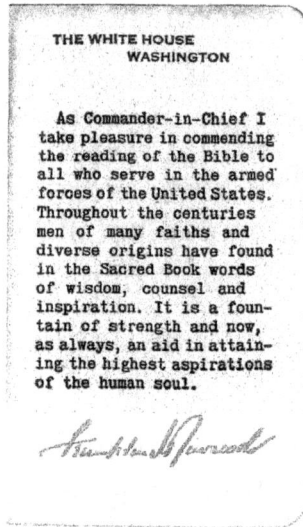

THE WHITE HOUSE
WASHINGTON

As Commander-in-Chief I
take pleasure in commending
the reading of the Bible to
all who serve in the armed
forces of the United States.
Throughout the centuries
men of many faiths and
diverse origins have found
in the Sacred Book words
of wisdom, counsel and
inspiration. It is a foun-
tain of strength and now,
as always, an aid in attain-
ing the highest aspirations
of the human soul.

President Roosevelt's cover letter when
issuing the Jewish Bible to the armed forces.

Albert celebrating
his bar mitzvah.

Jewish pocket Bible given to Army troops
by President Franklin Roosevelt. Albert
kept it in his pocket over his heart for three
wars and prayed it every night.

Family picture when Albert went to war at
age 17. Standing behind Rose, their mother,
are three sons: Murray, Herb, and Albert on
the right, the youngest.

CHAPTER 2

Basic Training Camp/ Miller Boys

March 10, 1944. Arrived at Camp Wheeler, Macon, Georgia, for eight weeks of basic training. I was to be in the AIT (Advanced Infantry Training). For my size and weight, it was decided that I would be a good heavy-weapons crew man, able to handle parts and heavy weapons.

One week while training, I found myself in a pit with three other soldiers practicing how to throw live grenades aiming at an old tank. One of the three was a slight Italian kid from New York. When he found it to be his turn, he pulled the pin and froze.

The grenade dropped out of his hand and down onto the floor of the pit. I quickly pushed him aside and shoved the grenade out of the pit. It exploded out of harm's way.

Corporal Nau, a Southern boy and one of the three in the pit standing near the Italian kid as he froze after removing the pin, realized I had only seven seconds to work with to save our lives. He recommended me for the Soldier's Medal. I was immediately promoted to Private First Class.

This was not a usual happening for 17-year-old recruits. This was one of the first of many miracles of protection to follow me through three wars as promised by the Lord.

The very next day, after the grenade incident and after a 15-mile march, I found my mother waiting for me. She waited in the day room while l showered and changed into a summer uniform to go to town.

We went to the Hotel Dempsey for dinner and she took a room for the night. I went back to basic training. At this point my mother knew l was not going to officer's training school. She did meet my new friends, the Miller boys, and the next morning she left. My mother told me not to do anymore "cockamamie" heroics.

April 16, 1944. Basic training is over at Camp Wheeler. I have been enjoying the company of the three Miller boys. They were not related. Abe Miller was married and Bob and Sid Miller were not. They were from northeast Philadelphia, Chicago, and New York.

Our last night in Camp Wheeler, there was a large-unit crap card game. We won $1800 that night and it was considered a lot of money for 1944. We were told that our next stop was to be Camp Livingston, Louisiana, to get our embarkation orders and assignments.

On route, there was a delay and instead we were given a 10-day leave. I got off the train in Newark and went home to Clinton Manor. Abe Miller got off in Philadelphia, Bob went to Chicago, and Sid to New York. I enjoyed my leave with family and my girlfriend in Newark. After the 10 days, myself and the Miller boys returned by train to Camp Livingston, Louisiana.

When we arrived at Camp Livingston, our respective units had already left. Some shipped out to Alaska and some sent here in the United States. We were told at Camp Livingston to wait for our new assignments and that new orders would be forthcoming.

Since it was the weekend, myself and the Miller boys were given two, three-day passes to New Orleans. After almost 10 days of gambling, there was nothing left of the $1800—not even for bus fare. We had to hitchhike back to base.

We were laughing and joking on our hike back, talking about our good times and our girlfriends. It was great hanging out with the Miller boys.

CHAPTER 3

The Miller Boys/Normandy Invasion

We received our orders at Camp Livingston, Louisiana. We were assigned to the 4th Infantry Division. We left the next day by train for Camp Kilmer, New Jersey. We would leave on a luxury ocean liner, the Queen Elizabeth. This was the original Queen Elizabeth. The stabilizers were shut off because they used too much power, so it was a week's ride full of sea sickness!

We were not told where we were headed, but because of the specific vaccinations we were given, we suspected it was Europe.

May 1, 1944. The Queen Elizabeth arrived in Ireland at night. We went to Newport, Essex, England, by train and then we divided up for one month. We were trained on embarkation, landing, etc. I was always with the Miller boys and glad to have found these good buddies—best buddies with a tight bond of friendship in this short time.

Myself and the Miller boys left from England with the 4th Infantry. We were headed for Normandy, France, for the Normandy Invasion.

There were 10,000 men in each division. In my company there were 200 men. There were two boats for Company K, 2nd Battalion, 4th Division, with one-hundred men in each boat. We attempted to board the LSIs (Land Ship Infantry).

I was the last to board the first boat. We were boarding alphabetically and I was the last to board for the letter L.

The Miller boys were the first to board the second LSI, beginning with the letter M. I wanted to be with my friends in the second boat. I was told to stay where I was, and I decided not to argue. The chaplain of our company, who was in the first boat, said I should just stay there.

We journeyed across the North Sea on the LSIs. I slept most of the overnight journey. In the early morning, the sun was coming up about 7:30 AM. June 6, 1944. All were praying and silent. I prayed my Jewish pocket Bible, Psalms 91 and 23. I continued to carry my Jewish pocket Bible over my heart for three wars. (The only exception was the march to the Battle of the Bulge. I knew that if ever I was captured by the Germans, I would be a dead man if they found my Jewish Bible.)

As the sun rose, I could see all the boats (10,000 men, a whole division), all different kinds of boats ready to land in different areas.

Ours was to land at Utah Beach so as to spread out the offensive. The second division was headed up by General Roosevelt, President Roosevelt's son. As my LSI was landing, I turned to look for my friends in the second boat. As I turned towards their boat, I saw the boat explode. All gone in an instant! (Later, I was told that it was not known if it was a sea mine, or our own artillery, or German artillery that caused the boat to explode.)

I felt sick, lost my bowels, and realized with whatever wisdom I could muster for my 17 years that, hey, this is not a football game. People are going to die. Maybe me. I stopped thinking and acted like a robot. All my friends gone in an instant! Not one survivor. All hundred men gone. I had wanted to be in that boat. I was wading chest deep in blood and body parts, trying to get to the beachhead.

When I did get there, I dug in and knelt down to pray. Captain Russell knelt down beside me.

He said, "Keep it together, son, tonight we will pray for those boys." He knew I was in shock and said a prayer with me.

After clearing the beachhead and climbing up the cliff with my gun and the bullet holster over my shoulder, I noticed Captain Russell and the first sergeant were going in the same direction. I helped move the machine gun to the left or to the right as he instructed me. I was scared, and I had the underwear to prove it.

We were now waiting for our unit to proceed when I had another nature call. I saw some hedge groves and as I walked around them, I came face to face with a young German soldier, not more than 15 years old who looked lost.

Maybe his unit had retreated. Was he alone along the hedge grove to perform a body function as well? Who knows. I reacted faster than he did. As he started to bring his gun up, mine was already out of the holster. No more than 25 feet between us.

I could see his face. I was a sharp shooter with a pistol. The boy never got to scream. I shot him right between the eyes and saw the top of his head blow off.

My Army 45 pistol made a big hole. At the sound of the shot, the captain came around and said, "Nice shot, son." I had killed my first German. I felt sick again. His face has haunted me all my life. Now every day, later into my eighties, maybe every month, I would dream of him, see his face, and relive it. Even in battle or killing in self-defense, it seems that there is an alarm that sounds in the soul.

A loud and daunting reverberating alarm, signifying that an important component of the creation code has been shattered and violated. A witness that the sanctity of life always rules.

Two weeks of fighting after Normandy, we met up with Patton's group going to Paris. Rather than walk, we hitched a ride on their tanks. We were told of the tremendous casualties suffered by the airborne divisions in Normandy.

They said airborne was looking for 200 pounders, six-feet tall to replace them. Jumping in combat from 500 feet, they needed big guys so that their weight plus the weight of the gear would promote a good and fast fall. I volunteered.

To be honest, my motives were not so much to help out with the airborne losses, but rather, I thought it would get me back to the states for airborne training. Maybe Fort Bragg or Fort Benning.

Well that wasn't the case. I was sent immediately to England for two-day jump school. Just two days! Enough time to take a shower, get different uniforms for airborne and a two week supply of clean underwear. (I had none in weeks, cutting a slit in my pants and making do. I had left my personal items, which included underwear, on the LSI, as it was too much to carry up the beachhead along with the weapons.)

I went on four training jumps—three daytime and one night training jump. Just as I learned how to fold my parachute, I was immediately sent back to France. I was to join the 82nd Airborne Division.

We fought the whole way to Paris. We met resistance the whole way. We had to slow down at times so we didn't outrun our supply route and gasoline. Two months later we took Paris and had to stop and get dressed for a victory parade.

We were given showers and new Eisenhower uniforms to wear. The "new" Eisenhower uniforms for the airborne soldiers to wear during the parade consisted of white scarves and white, nylon shoe laces for our boots. French girls were rushing to kiss us and handing us food—French bread and lots of wine. After the parade we had to return the uniforms, scarves, and shoe laces, and we were given other uniforms.

CHAPTER 4

Combat Jump/March to Ardennes/Chaplain Rescue

Our job with the 82nd Airborne Division was to jump ahead of the fighting forces to cut German communication lines. Later I became a jump master, that is, the last one to jump. That being the case, I decided not to carry my emergency chute, because being the last to jump found me lower than 500 feet. There was no time to activate it anyway. I also had to carry my Browning automatic rifle and personal items, so no room for my emergency chute.

My first combat jump was in the Ardennes, along the northern French border.

We landed on the ground with about 13 in our "stick," and collectively the other sticks totaled about 200 of us. We immediately experienced intense, heavy fire from the retreating Germans trying to get to the German border. Captain Russell of K Company was waiting for backup to clear the heavy resistance. Two scouts were sent out and the Germans allowed them to continue past them quietly without resistance, and then began the heavy automatic fire.

Both scouts were then shot. The chaplain, who was a Catholic priest, went out to give them the last rites. He was running as fast as he could, hunched over, not on a crawl to avoid the overhead bullets, snapping just a few feet off the ground.

He never got to the scouts as he was shot several times in the legs and thigh. He started screaming, "Help me, God, help me, God, save me."

Then screaming for his mother! This went on for a while and I could not stand it anymore.

Later I realized he was screaming for Mary, Mother of Jesus. I would have had no idea about that. How could a Jewish Orthodox boy no less, handle someone screaming for his mother! We have a special thing with our mothers. Well that was all I could stand. I told the captain I was going to get him. The Captain said don't go. Wait for the reinforcements to clear it for us. I said, sorry I can't stand it. I have to go get him.

There were 200 of us and myself the only Jew, and a Catholic priest no less, significant, due to my past experience with a Catholic priest. Priest or not, I had to get him.

I ventured out to get the chaplain on my belly in a crawl. I could hear the snapping of the bullets as they continuously whizzed overhead.

I finally arrived and gave the chaplain my morphine and a second shot of his own that we all carried. That was a heavy dose and I was hoping it would not kill him. I waited and rested while the morphine kicked in. He was hit in the thigh with blood all over. Both legs were shot and obviously he could not walk or crawl back!

I then started screaming and cursing him and calling him all kinds of names, saying that he was a stupid SOB and why did he do such a stupid thing by not crawling to avoid the bullets.

"Now I have to carry you back!"

The chaplain knew me, as I always went to his prayer meeting, and he knew I was the only Jewish one in the company.

I told him in an angry voice: "I will have to carry you back on my chest! One thing for sure, if I am going to get killed, you will be the first one on my chest to get the bullets."

I lifted him onto my chest and proceeded to inch my way back with my heels digging into the mud, inching back slowly, very, very slowly. It took almost an hour and a half total, up and back. The snapping of the bullets overhead was a sound I will never forget.

When I finally got back, I gave the chaplain to the medics and they put tourniquets on his wounds. He was full of blood, and so was I from carrying him on my chest. The captain was angry with me and I apologized and told him I was sorry, but that I could not stand his cries for help.

I did not think I would ever hear again about this priest, nor did I follow up on whether or not he survived. I did not have too much time to reflect on the ramifications of this drama with a Catholic priest no less, and what significance it would have in my life.

I found myself caught up now with our reinforcements arriving, and it wasn't long before the Germans ran low on ammunition and surrendered. About 150 Germans surrendered with lots of automatic rifles and machine gun pistols called P40s.

We had to continue the march, clearing the way through France. I had no thought that I would ever hear about or from this priest again. God had a surprise for me on both counts.

CHAPTER 5

Combat Jump/March to Bastogne/Out-of-body Experience

December 16, 1944. The Battle of the Bulge began. Today this will be my nineteenth combat jump with the 82nd Airborne. I saw so many boys die on these jumps to clear German communication centers. I saw Larry Eldridge from Trenton, New Jersey, do a Roman candle and die while jumping.

The mission today is to destroy the German communications center and get to Bastogne to defend the city and join the 102nd Division. They needed our weapons to help defend Bastogne.

We landed in a forest and began the march. This time I had a hunch that I should leave my Jewish Bible behind, along with my personal items, which included a letter to my parents if I did not survive. I had my little Browning automatic rifle and ammunition with me. Marching in the forest close to the German communications center, there was such a maze of communication wires. I knew we would never have time to cut them all. So I made an alternate choice. We would blow up the building.

We broke up our party of 13 and circled the building. Each group had enough plastic to plant. We lit a long fuse and left the area. We were heading for Bastogne when we heard the explosion. All my men patted me on the shoulder and gave me a closed fist. We marched towards Bastogne.

Marching, I stepped on a land mine, a "Bouncing Betty." They called it a Bouncing Betty because it was designed to bounce five feet in the air and blow your head off.

I felt it click as soon as I stepped on it and tried to do a back flip, so instead of blowing off my head, the mine blew my dog tags and ID into my chest. My face and other parts were wounded, including my left eye that was out of the socket and my right eye full of blood. I was blind and bleeding profusely from the chest and face wounds. Still conscious, I heard the company medic, Joe Fernando, say to the captain, "Al Lifschultz has less than five to ten minutes to live. What do you want me to do?"

They did not think I would make it, so on December 19, sometime before noon, they left me in a field with my rifle, helmet on top, with the bottle of plasma, and myself morphine medicated.

Just as they left, I felt some liquid
on my face. I was blinded, but I could
tell it was snow! Very softly it came
down in billows and in no time, I lost
consciousness and was completely buried
in snow. As it turned out, the snow
stopped the bleeding. I did not feel cold.
As I lay there covered in the soft snow, I
thought, what a good way to die.

I floated in and out of consciousness
throughout the night. Prayed. At
one point, I sensed that someone was
approaching me. Closer and closer,
and then the person said, "I am Zeder,
your grandfather." He did not have the
appearance of my grandfather as my
grandfather had a wooden leg, but he did
have a fatherly presence about him.

He said to me, "I cannot take you with
me right now. I love you, but I cannot
take you with me. It is not your time.
Also, if I take you now it will kill your
mother who is suffering already, and it is
not her time." With that he left.

Years later, I came to realize that because of my Jewish orientation, in our religion we had Yahweh who was God, not God the Father. After my Christian conversion, I believe that it was God, our Father, who had visited me to prepare me for what was to happen within hours.

In the morning, I saw myself floating over my body. I could see (even though I was blinded) a German soldier approach me, who began to stick me with the bayonet.

I was screaming at him to stop it! Stop it! But of course, he could not hear me. Then a German officer showed up and was looking at my papers. My dog tags and ID were embedded into my chest. For the first and only time, I had left my Jewish Bible behind. No tags or ID. He read my papers out loud and said to the other soldier, "Look! His name is Lifschultz. This is an old German name. He must be one of those German Americans."

The Lifschultzs were a long line of German warriors." The officer continued to read. "Says here he was born in Irvington, New Jersey. He must be one of those German Americans loyal to the Nazi party." I yelled: "That's not true! No way! I am not!" Of course, they could not hear me. Dad was right to move us out of there to Newark.

How strange that the German officer knew about Irvington, New Jersey. Then the officer said to the other German soldier, "Stop with the bayonet. This one is to be saved." The policy was not to take prisoners, much less dying ones, but the German officer then wrote on my papers a notation: "This one is to be saved."

I myself asked every German soldier I ran into thereafter to please give me a gun so that I could commit suicide, knowing they would kill me anyway if they found out I was a German Jew, and I did not want to live blind and without legs.

I was immediately taken to a small, German medical unit and then transferred by ambulance, no less!, to Heidelberg Hospital, Germany. All along the way, on presentation of my papers, I heard the comment: "This one is to be saved."

My parents were notified in the meantime that I was missing, and they held the traditional Jewish services for me and mourned that I was presumed dead. Later, after l left the hospital, they were advised that I was alive.

Nothing more.

I needed four eye operations, among other procedures. My doctor was very nice. He was a German captain who had a Jewish name, Oppenheimer. Usually a colonel would be the head surgeon, I was told. They operated on the shrapnel in my chest with a giant magnet. This was the only way they could get it out of my chest.

To this day, I still have the dog tags and ID imbedded in my chest and the shrapnel under both eyes. I have issues today with little vision and am bedridden due to the leg injuries.

During the first eye surgery, they cleaned up the right eye, and not until the fourth surgery when the doctor turned off the lights and leaving just one small light on, took off the bandages and asked me if I could see anything. I was able to get a glimpse. It was hard to focus, but I was on my way to recovering my eye sight.

I was filled with great emotion and joy. I knew that God was protecting me and that I would survive this. I would live. I was sure without a doubt that God had orchestrated all the events that led me to this German hospital and that He guided the surgeon's hand to make it happen.

CHAPTER 6

Heidelberg Hospital/POW Camp/Russian Rescue

January 8, 1945. Heidelberg Hospital, Germany.

The German hospital staff brought me a birthday cake and wished me a happy eighteenth!! Obviously, they still don't know I am Jewish. At the end of this month, after four operations to restore my eye sight and several procedures to remove the shrapnel in my chest, I was discharged to a Polish prisoner-of-war camp. The building was an abandoned boys school, so there were showers and a dining room to eat our three meals, which consisted of one ladle of greasy potato soup for all three meals.

When I arrived at the POW camp, the Germans in charge of prisoner intake were interrogating me for recent military information. I thought this was overkill, considering my short time involved with the war and not having any significant rank or status. The interrogation continued and finally as the German looked over my papers again, he said: "Look here! This kid, Lifschultz, has a royal German name. What is a good German boy doing fighting against the motherland?" he asked.

With that, I had no more patience for more interrogation and said, "Well, it was easy for me, you SOB. I am a smart-aleck street kid and I am Jewish!"

The German officer hit me on my right side and knocked me to the floor, where he and others started kicking me. I was thinking I would be killed right there on the spot, my first day at the POW camp.

The captain in charge of our POW company was Captain Edward Berlinsky. I knew this captain from high school.

He was a little guy, 5'4" and played football in high school. He was a senior when I was a freshman. He rushed over and threw himself over my body and yelled to the Germans to stop!

He said, "I know this kid. I cannot go back to New Jersey and tell his parents that he died like this. His parents own the biggest catering company in New Jersey and are well-known and respected. I just cannot let him die like this."

Well they stopped beating me and said I was to be assigned a job cooking for the German officers. So, I went from greasy potato soup to sausages, cheese, bread, ham, and some pretty good stuff.

The Germans gave me an oversized shirt to wear for this kitchen duty, and I proceeded to stuff this shirt every day after I cleaned up the tables with the leftovers from the German officers' tables.

I was able to eat all I wanted there and I could steal bread, sausages, ham and cheese, which I would stuff under my shirt and field jacket to bring to my fellow prisoners.

One day, as I was leaving the kitchen with my shirt stuffed with food, a German officer passed and we were required to salute them. An auto response, I quickly saluted and all the food fell out of my jacket onto the ground.

I was given another beating and fired from my cooking detail and sent back with the prisoners to greasy potato soup.

This time a new detail; myself and my angel, Captain Berlinsky, of all people, the one who saved me upon my arrival and responsible for the Germans assigning me to the officer's kitchen duty, was assigned to work garbage detail with me for the camp.

The first day of garbage detail, Captain Eddie would jump off the truck and pass upward the cans for me to dump down into the truck.

Our German guard who was an older, overweight and stocky man with a shotgun, was having difficulty pulling himself up to the top of the truck to mount his guard position. I extended out the palm of my hand to give him a lift up so he could take his position. He was having difficulty because of his weight and trying to hold onto his shotgun at the same time. I motioned for him to give me his shotgun, so I could help him up.

When he gave me his shotgun, I said, "You stupid SOB! I can kill you right now if I wanted to with your own shotgun."

Captain Eddie became almost hysterical. He screamed at me to give the shotgun back because if the German guards on the towers above saw this, they would kill us both. I gave the German guard back his gun, but instead of hurling him onto the top of the truck, I hurled him instead with a twist of the hoist up, causing him to go flying forward and sliding down into the pile of garbage.

We got fired and sent back to
confinement. Captain Eddie was furious.
He said, "Lifschultz, I am tired of dealing
with your death wish. It is getting to me.
Just stay on your side of the prison, and
I will stay on the other side until this is
over."

On April 16, 1945, we prisoners
woke up to complete silence. No guards
anywhere that we could see. All had
disappeared. We were afraid to venture
out of the prison in case they would be
waiting with machine guns to gun us
down.

Ten hours later, we were rescued by
Russian troops. Now I wanted to live. I
knew that I would survive.

The Russians greeted us kindly and
were very good to us. They deloused us,
cleaned our uniforms, and gave us Russian
underwear and warm clothing. They took
us back to Moscow by train, as it was still
not safe here with the Germans retreating.

On the train, a Russian officer made a comment to Captain Eddie, captain of the POW camp. The officer suspected me of being a turncoat because my body looked too well nourished while the other prisoners did not.

This was due to the rare treatment at the German hospital, and also from being assigned the first day of POW camp to German officers kitchen duty.

Well, Captain Eddie told the Russian officer, "He is absolutely not a turncoat! Just a fat kid."

May 8, 1945. The Russians treated us like royalty in Moscow. We were sent to an American hospital for checkups and treatment. They wined and dined us and put us in the best hotels and the best rooms in Red Square. I noted that these Russians were such a very loving, kind people and genuinely concerned. Of course, this was pre-cold war.

Nevertheless, again with what wisdom I could muster, now a young 18 year old, I came to the conclusion that people don't make wars, governments do.

CHAPTER 7

Paris Hospital/Pope Pius XII

Upon arriving in Paris, I was then sent to a hospital in Paris for a complete checkup as was everyone, and there waited for new orders as we all did. At the hospital, I met a young girl named Janette, and we dated. Her parents liked me a lot.

While at the hospital, I received orders from the State Department that I was going to the Vatican to see Pope Pius XII by a specific invitation from the pope. I said, "What do they want to see me about? I am just a corporal and why does he, the pope, want to see me?"

The orders from the State Department were specific, and I went along with it, thinking, I always wanted to see Italy, so why not. I had lots of cash from the money I received from the American Occupation Combat Troops Fund. I was given a jeep and a pass. Janette and I set out, and travelled over the French Alps to Italy. It took two or three days. I arrived in Rome and left Janette in a hotel room while I went to the Vatican.

I was introduced to the pope as follows: "This is the American Army Corporal who saved the life of our Catholic chaplain, who was badly wounded and rescued by Corporal Lifschultz."

The pope then said he wanted to thank me from the deepest part of his heart for risking my life to save one of his flock. The pope said that even though I was not of his faith, that he wanted to thank me and give me this set of rosary beads. He said, "At all times keep it with you. It will keep you safe."

I carried this rosary many miles and in future wars. It was kept in my Army men's kit and I still have it to this day. So the Catholic priest (Army chaplain) survived and now the priest of priests, the pope, thanks me? So totally startling! Looks like God has a plan for healing my horrendous childhood wound. More surprises to come.

Rosary given to Albert by Pope Pius XII
at the Vatican meeting.

Janette and I travelled around Italy and Spain and then went back to Paris for new orders. I was told that it would be a long wait. I would not go to Asia or Japan as rumors were suggesting, because it would take a while to reconstruct my records, for I was last listed as "missing in action."

I asked if there was any way to expedite this process and was told unfortunately not, unless I requested a discharge from the Army. Then I could be released earlier, if I joined the Army Reserve. I agreed. I wanted to see my family. I could not take Janette with me, but kissed her goodbye and left her a rich young girl with a potato sack full of the money that I had received from the American Occupation Combat Fund. I told her I would try to come back for her.

CHAPTER 8

Homebound/Marriage/ Reserves

I was then sent to Camp Lucky Strike in France, waiting for the Hood Victory ship to take me out of the Le Havre area straight across the Atlantic and home to be discharged. We pulled into New York Harbor. We then pulled out again due to rumors that we were to disembark in Boston, then Fort Dix for debriefing. I kissed the ground when once again on American soil.

September 1945. I arrived at Fort Dix and after debriefing, I was allowed to go home the next day.

I was glad l opted for the Reserves since it would have taken awhile for new orders with the crowd of soldiers awaiting new orders in France. I left the next morning from Fort Dix with my mother, father, and grandmother, who had travelled the 70 miles to pick me up.

We were reunited and so glad to see each other. The last notice they received was that I was missing in action, and later that I was alive with no other details.

We had lots of catching up to do. Mom was more of a synagogue person and more orthodox than my father. He just was glad to leave the kosher area where they lived and get a nice ham steak and eggs. I told my mother about Janette.

She said to take my time as there were a lot of local girls coming through and around the catering business, and that many were very beautiful and Jewish.

She said I would be helping with the business and this could happen. I agreed to wait.

I told Mom about the pope, but she did not think much about it. My dad, on the other hand, was eager to announce to all his Irish friends at the Elks club about the honorary meeting with the pope and the rescue of the Catholic chaplain. Dad was impressed that I got the Silver Star and the Purple Heart for shrapnel wounds. He already knew I received the Soldier's Medal in boot camp. He told everyone about my meeting General Patton at a medical clinic while I was being treated for shrapnel wounds.

The general asked me with a big smile, showing his mouth full of cavities, "Soldier, how did you get the Silver Star?" I think I was trying to promote a sense of modesty and I mumbled, "Not sure sir."

The general gave me a big slap on the back that almost brought me to the floor, and he said, "Well, son, if I was to get the Silver Star, I would certainly know why."

His soldier assistant then proceeded to give every wounded soldier the Purple Heart. I was put in for the Medal of Honor, but already I received the Silver Star instead.

I thought I would relax and hang out with my brother Murray, but found out later he was engaged to be married, so we did not have much time to hang out.

I wanted to go back to school. When I went back to complete my high school diploma, as I had only the war diploma, I met of all people, my angel, Captain Eddie, who saved my life at POW camp. He was teaching and also the football coach. I got to play football too, and even played Notre Dame.

Then I went on to Pratt Business School and received a degree in business administration in 1950.

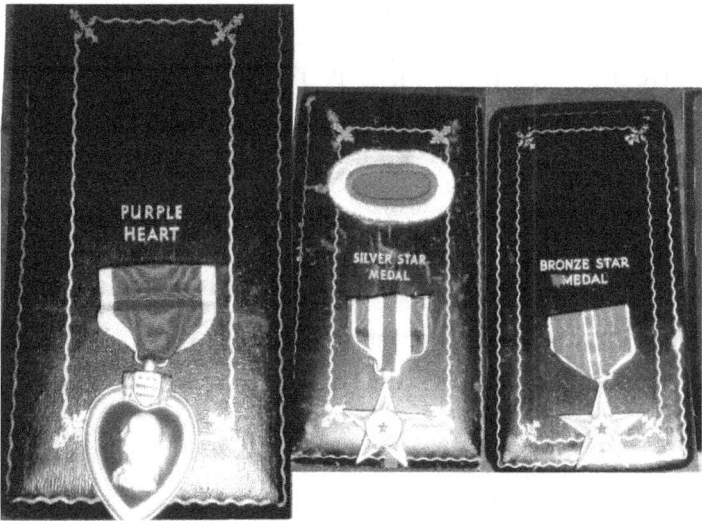

Albert's medals from left to right: Purple
Heart, Silver Star, and Bronze Star.

Two medals from the Korean War for
50 air sorties flown in combat.

I was working with the family business when I met my wife, Mimi, who became an accomplished opera singer. Mom was right. A lot of beautiful girls hung out around the business. I started dating Mimi in 1947. We dated for several years. We had a lot in common. She was staying with my family at the Clinton Manor. Her father owned a hotel and we shared the love of opera.

I got to sing with her often and later she was at the Met in New York, where I sang and joined her on several occasions.

I had been very busy with college and night school, training also with the Reserves all at the same time. My college experience was very disappointing, as I found out I had very little in common with the other students and felt out of place because of my previous war experiences.

I was close with my brother Murray because of his military experience as Army medic. My brother Herb, who was a polio victim, could not get into the military. He was distant and did not live long. Murray lived to age 92.

Now, I was able to use the GI Bill to complete training as well. I had purchased an old airplane and received my instrument training for single-engine aircraft, while meeting with the Reserves on weekends.

This airplane was a joke. I had purchased it from Army surplus. A B13 for $275.00 with full instruments. The gas tank would burn 100 gallons of gas an hour. Top speed 120 miles an hour. Every ride used 50/60 gallons of gas in one half hour! However, it served my purpose very well as I was able to use it for instrument rating as well as to secure my single-engine pilot license.

I continued to work at the family business and married Mimi in April 1950. It was a large wedding with over 350 people, with some family, but most were opera stars. I continued with my interest in opera, practicing with Mimi. No babies yet.

Just six months after the wedding in 1950, while I was off with the Reserves at summer camp at Pine Camp, New York (later to be named Ford Drum), I was told to get my gear ready and to report for deployment from Indiana (Camp Atterbury).

I called my wife to tell her from Pine Camp that I was being activated and was called out of the Reserves to go to the war in Korea. This was unexpected and with short notice. The Army was aware that I had completed instrument training and had a single-engine and instrument license. They were eager to activate me to Korea for air combat.

CHAPTER 9

Army Aviator Reserves/ War in Korea

The summer of 1950, I was activated and checked out by Army Aviation. I was placed with an artillery unit as air spotter with the 28th Division, Artillery Headquarters Company. I was then a sergeant and promoted to master sergeant. I was put in for warrant officer.

I flew 25 sorties, then extended for another 25 sorties. I received two air medals later, after flying over 50 flights, and my airplane was falling apart.

The bullets came through the plane and it was dangerous to fly and had to be serviced. The plane was worn out and so was I.

I was back on the ground and observing with binoculars on a hill above the Yalu River in Korea where there was a huge battle going on. The Chinese were walking over their dead. Blood everywhere. A gruesome scene.

Suddenly a shell hit about 100 yards away from where I was standing. It was close enough to cause the hill I was standing on to collapse. The ground gave way under me and I fell injuring my knee and back. I was put into a cast and discharged back home.

In 1951, I was discharged. I caught a plane from Washington to Newark. I decided to surprise my wife Mimi, who was performing in the Opera, Madame Butterfly, at the Met in New York.

We had practiced this opera and others so many times before. I sang in the Broadway show, Carousel, and had previously sung at the Met when I was at Pratt Business School. In elementary school, I sang the Lord's Prayer, and also at graduation.

My voice changed in high school to tenor, so I was then suited for light opera. I wanted to sing with Mimi. I arrived in secret and was permitted to practice my part, which I could play in my uniform. Max Gutman, who was agent impresario at the Met, helped me pull it off. He made it possible for me to practice in a private room. I was on time for the matinee. When I appeared on stage in the first act, which allowed me to be dressed in my uniform, Mimi hardly recognized me. She was surprised. It was a great performance and very romantic. That night my first child, Stewart, was conceived.

Afterwards, I was sent to Walter Reed Hospital for a checkup and therapy.

Every day l read a different book at Walter Reed Hospital. I was very impressed with the book, *Michel, Michel*, by Robert T. Lewis. One part of the book got my attention. It was the story of an infant born to Jewish parents when the Nazis occupied Germany.

The boy was raised by a Catholic woman who was unable to have children. She raised the boy, after his Jewish parents were exterminated by the Nazis.

Later, the Jewish relatives came from Israel to claim the child from his Catholic home. She refused to give him up. There was a court fight and the judge addressed the boy and asked him two questions. The first: Do you believe in Jesus Christ? And the second: Do you believe that He is your Messiah?

The boy answered yes to both questions. The judge said, "Well then, you are a Christian," and ordered the boy be allowed to stay with his Catholic family.

Days later, I stopped a rabbi at Walter Reed Hospital and told him about what I read, and that I too had come to believe in Jesus Christ as well. The rabbi said, "Well, that would make you a Messianic Jew."

For a long time afterwards, I tried church after church, trying to find out where I belonged. I went to every denomination and found I did not fit in with the Protestant churches, including Episcopal, even though I was a lead singer at most of their services.

CHAPTER 10

Las Vegas Job/Divorce/ Pentagon Job/Viet Nam

Mimi was travelling all over the world with opera groups and her agent. I found myself still in the Army Reserve and working the family catering business. Now a father of two. Bonnie, the second child, was born in 1961.

I moved the family to Las Vegas where I took a position with food and beverage management at a noted hotel. My wife was singing at the Sands Hotel. Bonnie was now five years old and Rosegale was born in 1965. Mimi moved out and we were divorced in Las Vegas.

She walked out on the three children and we were all upset, including Mimi's mother, who offered to take care of the three children at our house in New Jersey.

My brothers at this time were successful in elbowing me out of the family business. Now wounded by my brothers, this festered with me for years. Very hard to forgive them, as at the time, I found myself desperately in need of work to support the family.

In 1967, I was with the Army Reserve, Horsham, Pennsylvania. I heard of a course offered by the Army Food Conference and became an Army food advisor after 10 weeks of training at Fort Lee, Virginia. I was then sent to work at the Pentagon, a job which would allow me to support my family.

At this time, I was able to take advantage of flight training in helicopters and was upgraded to CW3 status with the Army Reserve.

My work at the Pentagon as a food advisor entailed rewriting and introducing new regulations to deter and avoid large amounts of food that were being wasted. Tons of food were being discarded after training camp and weekend drills, including Reserve maneuvers.

I introduced changes and additions to the AR 30-1 Food Service Manual. It was to be noted that all unused food would be sent to orphanages, senior centers, and schools in those specific areas.

This was successfully implemented along with other suggestions to avoid waste in the purchase of more efficient kitchen equipment. While I was still working at the Pentagon, I applied and was accepted at Fort Rucker, Alabama, for helicopter training. I completed a four-week course and now became certified to fly a Loach helicopter and Huey helicopter (light and medium helicopters).

In 1969 at work in the Pentagon, I was told of a food advisor stationed in Viet Nam who lost his wife and children in a car accident and needed to be relieved to go back home. This touched my heart, hearing of this food advisor's great loss. I volunteered to relieve the food advisor in Viet Nam on a TDY (temporary duty detail).

I arrived in Viet Nam on Thanksgiving Day in 1969. I was immediately assigned mortuary duty. The food advisory job became secondary to this additional duty. It was a very active American Infantry Division. There were a lot of casualties.

Christmas Eve in Viet Nam found me flying a helicopter to deliver food behind enemy lines. Something I was glad to do. I was shot down and then rescued by our troops, who appreciated what I was doing with the Christmas delivery.

I had to demolish the helicopter, so the enemy would not be able to use it. I suffered neck and back injuries and was sent home.

The end of 1969 finds me home from Viet Nam and now back with the Reserves in the Pentagon. I reported in and was sent back to my home base with the 157th Infantry Brigade at Horsham, Pennsylvania.

General Harry Mier was now Adjutant General of the Pennsylvania National Guard and was looking forward to my transfer to the Guard. I was in Horsham from 1969-1972. My transfer came through with General Mier in 1972 at Indiantown Gap, Pennsylvania.

I met and married my second wife, Renee, there.

To Al Lifschultz
    alias the Big Dipper
A great guy and truly professional
soldier and one whom I consider a
personal friend and confidant.
    Best wishes always
        Harry Mier

Major General Harry Mier, Adjutant General
of the Pennsylvania National Guard with
message to Albert, 1972.

CHAPTER 11

Death of Wife Mimi and Daughter Rosegale

Since I was stationed at the Indiantown Gap in Pennsylvania with the National Guard, I decided to rent a house there so Renee could come to visit. She was trying not to retire until age 60 so she could collect her pension that she worked all these years to receive. She was looking forward to her retiring and our new full-time life together.

In 1970, I received word that my ex-wife Mimi and my little four-year-old daughter, Rosegale, were both dying in the same hospital in Newark, New Jersey.

Mimi had last stages of Hodgkin's disease and Rosegale was dying with a terminal stage of Leukemia! With both Rosegale and Mimi dying so young and together, would have brought me down for sure. It would surely have rendered me unable to be there for them. God was once again giving me the strength and courage to function and to be there for them now. I do not know to this day how I was able to do this, but God gave me the strength to hold on.

As Mimi lay there dying, worrying about our little girl, I was filled with so much compassion for Mimi as I watched her suffer her own early death.

It was a wrenching pain, not to be consoled. I felt her pain. I was so moved and overwhelmed suddenly with forgiveness for her. The forgiveness overflowing and drowning my soul in sorrow.

Finally, with floods of sorrow in my soul, I found the ability to forgive her and myself. Like a wounded animal, I went off alone to lick my wounds of sadness and affliction.

I was with Rosegale when she passed. I was holding her hand. Her last words were, "God wants us to forgive." Her last words haunted me for years. Took me several years to process. I wrote a poem late 2011 entitled "Rosegale." I was then at last finally able to put it all together. Like any other human, I went through an intense mourning process with thoughts of self-incrimination, anger, and desperation.

I had seen way too much death in the three wars. A lot of them young kids. This pain was worse. Even the pain of seeing my young friends, the Miller Boys, die as I watched, and the young German soldier I shot at Normandy, whose face haunted me every day until age 86.

By then, it was only once a month instead of every day that I was subjected to nightmares. Even so, those were not as intense as the early deaths together of my ex-wife and little daughter.

When Rosegale passed, I tried to collect myself to go upstairs at the hospital to Mimi's room. She was in pain and under heavy medication, but she inquired as usual, "How is Rosegale?" I did not have the heart to tell her that she had just died, but said something about her being in remission.

This time the visit from the angel of death was devastating and left me defeated, unable to recover.

CHAPTER 12

Pennsylvania Flood Rescue/Hurricane Agnes

Two months after the deaths of Mimi and Rosegale, I was back with the National Guard at Indiantown Gap, Pennsylvania. I was called after Hurricane Agnes in 1972 to head up the rescue of some 80,000 victims who survived the flood. They had lost everything and were now homeless, left with absolutely nothing!

I arrived in Wilkes-Barre to assist with the feedings and shelter. When I arrived, I witnessed pandemonium and confusion. No one knew what to do with all the donations of food, clothing, tents, and trailers that were sitting in the field in piles.

I was asked to sort and organize the relief effort. I was up for 72 hours nonstop as the donations continued at the airport between Wilkes-Barre and Scranton, Pennsylvania. I noticed one runway not being used for air traffic and immediately ordered that a clothing station, grocery store, and medicine station be set up on this runway. All donations were sitting in piles in a field, and I immediately ordered the tents and trailers to be set up as soon as they arrived.

I organized the groceries with canned goods in one section, and canned meats, soups, and condiments organized in their own section. Food cooked and otherwise sorted for all to choose from. The donated clothing by size and gender. One section for baby food, powder and diapers, and baby clothing organized in another section.

After I completed this relief station on the unused paved runway, I was called to the town of Kingston where there was a football stadium downtown. I set up another relief station there.

These flood victims were my neighbors. My house was in Indiantown Gap not far from the disaster area. I felt driven and I operated in a frenzy mode, pulling from the resources available. I was trying to keep my focus and find every way at my disposal to relieve their suffering. Looking back, I believe I was responding to my own sense of loss from the deaths of Mimi and Rosegale and still aching in pain from my devastating losses.

Albert with General Mier at Indiantown Gap, Pennsylvania, flood of 1972.

Medal of Commendation for Albert's meritorious performance and leadership. Presented by Brigadier General William Gallagher for the operation to distribute food and supplies to 80,000 homeless flood victims during the flood disaster of 1972 caused by Tropical Storm Agnes.

My God had found a way to heal me, using my up-front personal witness of this flood's devastation and the tremendous loss and the needs of these 80,000 survivors. I saw there was something I could do here to help others with their extreme loss. It was pretty "text book" for God's way of doing things. I didn't get it at the time and just went with my gut-wrenching desire to help.

DEPARTMENT OF THE ARMY
HEADQUARTERS, FIRST UNITED STATES ARMY
FORT GEORGE G. MEADE, MARYLAND 20755

AHACG

SUBJECT: Letter of Commendation

THRU: The Adjutant General
Commonwealth of Pennsylvania
Department of Military Affairs
Annville, Pennsylvania 17003

TO: Chief Warrant Officer Albert I. Lifschultz
Headquarters & Headquarters Detachment
Pennsylvania Army National Guard
Annville, Pennsylvania 17003

1. While serving as Food Advisor to the Pennsylvania Army National Guard during the recent flood disaster caused by Tropical Storm Agnes, you distinguished yourself through meritorious performance of duty.

2. Your leadership of an operation to distribute food and supplies to 80,000 homeless flood victims greatly helped to alleviate their suffering and resulted in significant financial savings to the United States government. Assuming control of a chaotic and undermanned distribution center, you demonstrated exceptional leadership and organizational ability. The four major distribution centers and the supply lines you established resulted in efficient distribution of the large quantity of food and cleaning supplies rushed to the area. Your dedication and selfless performance was in the highest traditions of the military service, and reflects great credit upon yourself and the United States Army.

C. E. HUTCHIN, JR.
Lieutenant General, USA
Commanding

Letter of Commendation from Department of the Army to Chief Warrant Officer Albert I. Lifschultz for meritorious service for leading the operation to distribute food and supplies to 80,000 homeless flood victims, which greatly helped to alleviate their suffering and resulted in significant financial savings to the US government.

CHAPTER 13

Meeting Rescued Chaplain/ Catholic Conversion

Still with the National Guard, living at Indiantown Gap in Pennsylvania, I was requested by General Mier to drive him to the Cathedral in Harrisburg, Pennsylvania, for a Catholic service. I sat patiently through the whole service and listened. I crossed myself at the proper time. Then the bishop announced he was changing his homily.

He started by saying, "You all know I have a slight limp." My ears perked up. He said, "I received my limp in World War II from machine gun bullets."

He proceeded to tell the story of how he got wounded when he attempted to give last rites to the advance group of the 9th Regiment, K Company, 4th Division. He said he was rescued by a young soldier! To my surprise, he introduced me as the young soldier and had me stand up and told everyone that this was the brave kid that had saved him on the battlefield.

He looked at me and said, "Yes, this brave kid spoke so many 'kind' words to me while he was carrying me on his chest to safety!" (Tongue in cheek, he said this. I did not know that he had heard all my cursing and swearing at him for that long, one hour and a half rescue.)

He seemed very pleased with me and told me that he walks with a limp, but was so very grateful for his rescue. General Mier himself looked pleased with the results of this surprise meeting.

After the Catholic service with the Harrisburg bishop, we were invited to the reception in Hershey, Pennsylvania.

I decided on my way back from the church, to stop at camp and pick up the rosary that Pope Pius XII had given me and which I always had with me. I brought it to the reception at Hershey. I had no idea that General Mier had ordered such a magnificent buffet.

I showed the bishop the rosary and explained how I received it from the pope. He told everyone from the diocese at the reception that I received the rosary from Pope Pius XII as a thank you for saving him on the battlefield.

I told the bishop that the pope had told me to keep it with me always for protection, and that I had always kept this rosary with me which kept me safe through three wars. The bishop kissed it and blessed it.

Again, the hand and a word from the Father that he was continuing with the healing of my priest-inflicted wound as a young child.

The chaplain had survived death from his wounds, and with his rescue was alive and well. No coincidence for me that he happened to be a "Catholic" chaplain assigned to our division. It was revealed to me that not only was he alive and well, but a bishop now in the Catholic Church.

God did not allow my hate for Catholic priests to keep me from risking my life to save a brave chaplain who went out to administer the last rites under heavy German fire to those two wounded scouts. This courageous young chaplain, a newly ordained Catholic priest, was faithful to his calling and duty as a priest.

I was more than overwhelmed to learn that he had survived, and no less now a Catholic bishop.

It took me a while to digest this surprise meeting with the rescued chaplain. No coincidence that he was in Harrisburg, Pennsylvania, and myself in the National Guard stationed at nearby Indiantown Gap.

I remembered back to my association with him with our division, as he was the only chaplain assigned to us, and I the only Jewish soldier in that company. I marveled and was at the same time embarrassed to learn now that he heard all my angry cursing and mumbling directed toward him, while I carried him back at a slow crawl on my chest.

I believe that God indeed had a plan and that this healing was in the plan along with the other healings now in progress. My little girl, Rosegale, on her death bed said to me, "God wants us to forgive."

I had a lot to forgive and more to be angry about, with my children who died at a very young age and I a witness to all those young friends of mine that would die in three wars.

I had been very angry with God when the abuse happened to me in elementary school because I knew I was a good kid.

I was convinced after the abuse, that I was not a good kid, but a bad kid to have allowed this abuse to happen and go unpunished. A sentiment that I discovered most victims of abuse are found to be dealing with, and also the unexplainable and unwarranted guilt and anger I exhibited. I carried this unforgiveness for a long time. The anger had grown and remained a part of me for fifty years.

I realize now how very angry I was with God, and remembered that I refused to go to Hebrew school after the abuse. I would only consent to a verbal, abbreviated bar mitzvah ceremony. Well, I thought, Where were you God?

Catholic Conversion

In 1979, I resigned from the National Guard and the Reserves and took a job at a country club in the greater Johnstown area of Pennsylvania as a food manager.

I was introduced to Father Ronald O'Shinski at a dinner. He had been active in the Philippines and served as Air Force chaplain in the war. We became good friends and had many long discussions about the ways of God, about religion and where I fit in as a Messianic Jew.

I told him everything and included the experience with the abusive priest at age 8. I told him about volunteering for World War II at age 17 and of my rescue encounter with the Catholic chaplain and my risking my life to save him. Also, I told him about my encounter after the war with the priest of all priests, Pope Pius XII, and the Vatican experience. I recounted the surprise encounter with the rescued chaplain which had just occurred and how it was an eye opener regarding God's plan. I knew that God was obviously listening and directing my steps to heal this festering wound. I was still reading my Jewish Bible every night, Psalms 23 and 91.

I now know that God was listening and how His mercy and protection were with me all along.

I told Father Ron about my search from church to church to find my place, and how l just did not seem to fit in with the many denominations I experienced.

Father Ron asked how I felt about the Catholic Faith after all these happenings. I told him I wanted to become a Catholic. Father Ron gave me personal, religious-instruction classes (CCD) and afterwards personally baptized me when it was completed. I was now ready for the next step: first confession and first communion.

Father Ron reminded me that it was imperative for my soul that I forgive all those who had harmed me, and that meant the abusive priest too. My little girl, Rosegale, was at it again. (God wants us to forgive.) Her words now sounding in my soul. It has just been a few years after she uttered them on her death bed.

I asked the Lord and my little girl, who was in heaven, to help me to forgive. With the help of Rosegale and the mercy of God, I was now officially able to put my unforgiveness to rest.

Rosary given to Albert by Pope Pius XII
at the Vatican meeting.

CHAPTER 14

Retirement to Florida

In 1981, I opened a deli restaurant called Lox Stock and Bagel in Deerfield Beach, Florida. Soon I realized that it was not going to happen in the area. I closed it shortly thereafter, and I was hired by a medical courier company.

I was notified towards the end of 1985 that my son, Stuart, had been involved in a motorcycle accident and required surgery for his knee.

The surgery was successful, but my young son was found dead in the morning. He had aspirated as a result of the anesthesia. Literally suffocated by his own vomit from the anesthesia.

This was hard for all of the family. I was now mourning my son. He was dead at 31.

My wife, Renee, retired and joined me in Florida in 1987. While shopping for our new home, we looked at the new model villas at Deerfield Independence Bay and moved there to start our new life together with our little dog. I plunged myself into the medical courier business from 1987 to 2008. Cash was readily available, and I was earning $1500 a week.

My gambling addiction accelerated. It was serious, but I told no one, and seemed powerless to do anything about it. I became very depressed because it was getting increasingly difficult to pay the bills.

Renee was in and out of nursing homes. I saw her lung condition continue to deteriorate over these years. She was in and out each time for longer stays at the nursing homes.

During these times, I visited her every day, but it was hard, as my own health was deteriorating as well. I had not opened my Bible and was not praying much at all. I was totally preoccupied with my addiction.

Now, due to my old knee injuries, l was forced to use a wheelchair. I had to travel with my electric wheelchair and ordered a custom vehicle designed to pull and release the wheelchair so that I could function. When I thought things could get no worse, my medical courier company lost the contract that I was servicing after 17 years without notice and without any reason or explanation as to why they were cancelling.

My little dog died, and I was advised that Renee would never leave the nursing home as her lung condition rendered her non-ambulatory and her invalid status was to be her norm.

I myself was getting help with nurses and in and out of the Veterans hospital. No wife, no dog, no job.

During this time, my only remaining daughter, Bonnie, came to visit. She was still very bitter about her life and her lot with me as her father. I was very sick and I gave my daughter power of attorney. I was multiplying red blood cells, and they didn't expect me to live. Bonnie, with power of attorney, took almost all of my savings, and I asked her to leave. I thought, oh well, I would gamble it away for sure, if I survive. So, let her enjoy it.

With my cash gone, I could not gamble and had no chance of making money to support my habit. I succumbed to depression and thought the only way out was to kill myself.

I took my gun off the storage shelf where I had it stored with other unpacked items, and pulling the gun off the shelf, along with it came my little pocket Bible. It flew off the shelf and hit me on the head.

My head, now so full of depression and defeat that I could not process the message that God was obviously sending me! I took the gun and loaded it with one bullet and went to a secluded place and pulled the trigger. The gun was jammed and would not fire, and since I had only one bullet anyway, I returned home.

I took the gun for repair and was told that there was nothing wrong with it! I thought this is really, yes, really bad luck!

With Renee now terminal, I was involved each day with her critical condition. I tried to comfort her as much as I could and reminded her about God's mercy.

Ironically, I was unable to grasp this thought for myself. I loved her and now she was leaving me too.

CHAPTER 15

The Message and the Messenger

My own physical condition worsened. I was using the wheelchair with the car outfitted, so I could haul it around more often. I was still struggling to pay for food, gas, etc., and was working at a nearby car repair shop. I managed to get a reverse mortgage too. The shop owner gave me work here and there, picking up parts and helping with the bookwork and parts orders. It was not too far from my house. The owner and his wife were very kind and prepared food for me as well as helping me out with car repairs.

I was hanging out at the front desk computer at the repair shop one day when I noticed this woman sitting alone in the only waiting area offered by the shop. The area was empty of customers. She was patiently reading something, and I was absorbed with computer work.

The owner walked in and stated, "Wow, Al, you are looking so well for a man that was left for dead and came back to life." We discussed a few more things that he wanted me to do and left.

About thirty minutes or so later, the little lady got up and approached me saying, "Excuse me, sir." (I had my Army cap on, she not knowing thought she should address me as sir.)

"I heard what the owner commented about how you were left for dead and came back. I may be so out of line to ask you this, but did you see or hear anything or did you happen to have an out-of-body experience?"

She said she was Catholic and apologized again not knowing if I was a Christian or believed in a God or heaven. I told her that I too am Catholic and yes, that I did have an out-of-body experience. I believe I did get a visit from heaven. She smiled and seemed pleased and introduced herself as Vera Marie Verna and asked if l would share my experience.

I told her that I was mortally wounded from stepping on a land mine in World War II and left for dead. I recounted my out-of-body experience, bleeding out, and left in a wooded field. I heard the medic reporting to the company commander that I had less than 10 minutes to live. She listened intently when I recounted that, sometime after, a snow storm began and how I could feel it covering my body, stopping further bleeding.

I described what I had heard and seen that night, not realizing I was in an unconscious state. I could hear and see even though I was unaware of being blind and unable to speak.

She was taken back when I described how I was found in the morning by German soldiers who were attempting with a bayonet positioned on my back to end my life. I heard the German company commander ordering them to stop! He noticed my German name on my orders. He thought me to be of royal German warrior stock, not a German Orthodox Jew. He immediately ordered me to be sent by ambulance to Heidelberg Hospital in Germany. After several operations, my eye sight was restored and my injuries totally addressed.

I told her that I volunteered with the Army at age 17 and was part of the Normandy invasion and that I was forced, in self-defense, to shoot and kill a young German boy at close range.

I told her that for more than 50 years, every day, I would have nightmares about the German boy, who appeared younger than myself. Haunted, I would see his face and relive the trauma.

Vera Marie asked me if I had ever thought of publishing my out-of-body experience and the traumatic experiences from having to kill in defense of our country? I told her no, I did not. I never thought of myself as a hero at all, since I saw so many heroes along the way in three wars who died defending our country. She said she thought my story would be a powerful witness to the sanctity of all life, and to the traumatic long-term consequences of killing another, for whatever reason.

I noticed Vera Marie had tears in her eyes. I did too after she had me reliving these painful experiences, which I had not discussed with many others. I asked her, "Who are you anyway, that you were able to open me up like a tin can?"

She told me that she was very involved with pro-life issues. She was a director of a non-profit that rescues pregnant girls and helps destitute seniors requiring care and housing.

She went on to say that pro-life Catholic architects, (pro bono), were in the process of finishing a design for her non-profit. It is to be an intergenerational care center. It would include a maternity house, an assisted living facility (ALF), and a child care center on one campus. The center is to be oriented to respect life from conception to natural death. She said she had been trying for years to get HUD and other funding, but still not successful.

She went on to say that she is a single mother of three adopted children, who were offered to her unexpectedly. She said she will be eternally grateful to those mothers who chose to have these children, despite their desperate circumstances. The experience promoted a passion for her work to respect life from womb to tomb.

Vera Marie apologized for the tears, and for getting so emotional. She explained that her pet rabbit, Mr. Emily, had just died after 15 years of service to pro-life work. She said the Florida Catholic newspaper did a several page article about him with his pictures and those of her son with Roxie, their pet dog. Both pets had participated in pro-life activities to schools and nursing homes.

I told her that my faithful old dog, Shatzie, just died too and that my dear wife was now dying in a nursing home after her long stay there. It was so hard watching her suffer so much.

Vera Marie and I were both now unable to control the tears. With that, the owner of the auto shop came in to advise Vera Marie that her car was ready. He noticed both of us crying and said, "What in the world is going on here?" As she was trying to find some tissues, unable to speak, I mumbled something like, "We were sharing the loss of our old pets, who just died." He gave a strange look and left the room.

By now, it was getting late and Vera Marie said she had to leave to pick up her children at school. We exchanged contact information to call later. I stopped her from leaving and asked her to answer a very important question that had been troubling me for a while.

I thought she would be the person that would have an answer, considering our conversation.

I told Vera Marie that I was having severe financial difficulties since my company contract after 17 years was cancelled with no reason or explanation as to why I was dismissed. I told her I had asked God for an answer, but with no reply.

It seemed I was having very bad luck and now my wife dying at this time in the nursing home and our home having been in danger of foreclosure because of sudden loss of income. Why would God allow this bad luck? I asked.

Vera Marie looked very intent and, after a few minutes, asked me what kind of business was it?

I told Vera Marie that it was a medical courier company that for over 17 years I was hired to pick up dermatology samples. The majority were aborted fetuses from clinics and medical offices in all Palm Beach County, Dade and Broward Counties, and to transport them to a laboratory to be checked for missing fetal body parts that may have been left in the mothers after their procedures.

If the aborted fetus was missing parts, then the laboratory would then report immediately to the women's care centers and the offices that performed the abortion to notify the mothers for "recall," as it was now required that infant parts and fetuses were to be picked up and checked to see if the clinics and abortionists left any body parts in the mothers.

This was necessary as this situation was causing serious harm and even death to some of the women due to parts left inside after their procedures, especially partial birth abortions.

As I was recounting this, Vera Marie's face was gripped with a painful look of horror. She remained silent and, after some minutes of hesitation, which seemed more like an hour to me, she said, "I do have an answer for you. A very obvious answer considering what you have shared with me today. Al, this was no bad luck that your medical courier contract was cancelled. Your Father who visited you to save your life on various battlefields has been very impressed with your risking your life in three wars to save others. You told me you were haunted for years by the faces of those you were forced to kill."

She continued, "You realized that taking a life even in war and in self-defense is a serious and haunting issue. The sanctity of life is real. All life from conception to death is sacred.

This was no bad luck. This was your lucky day when God saw that you could not give up this job, so He had to do it for you! To stop you from participating in the business of the culture of death. I am surprised that it took all those years for Him to finally say, 'Enough!'"

She answered my question with such authority that the answer stunned me, as if by a powerful stun gun.

I replied, "Yes. I see that is very true. I will tell you why it took so long. Ten years into the business, I was making a stop at a clinic that always had more fetuses to pick up than others.

"This time, the fetuses were loaded in jars of formaldehyde and in covered bags onto my truck as usual. I went off in a hurry to get to the next stop. I had to cover 200 miles a day.

"While driving, I looked down, over to the area by the passenger seat, and with horror now observed an almost full-term baby boy, that I am sure did not fit into the usual small fetus jars of formaldehyde.

He was so big that he was in what
appeared to be a large pickle jar, without
a covering bag like the others. I don't
know how I missed it! When I looked
down I had to stop the car in a hurry to
vomit. I saw the baby so visible in this
large jar. I could see his little hands and
nose and feet. He was definitely a late-
term one, which I had not encountered
before. He was so perfectly formed that it
hit me.

"These are babies! Not tissue. These
are babies, innocent babies. I could
hardly continue my route. I tried to hire
someone else to do it for me, but it did
not work out. At this point I knew it was
wrong. This was not fetal tissue I was
transporting, but human babies.

"I was getting $1500 a week and my
gambling addiction had become severe.
Along with expenses for the nursing
home for my dying wife and paying my
mortgage, I was unable to give up the
contract because of my addiction. I tried

for years to resign, but continued for several more years until my company contract was cancelled just recently.

"I did not understand the 'why' and thought it was bad timing and my bad luck. I must thank you for opening my eyes to my blindness of God's hand of mercy that ended this nightmare for me."

Yes. I can see why God could not tolerate my continuing with this business and that I was blessed that He would not allow me to continue as a slave to my gambling addiction. No money, no gambling. I told Vera Marie that she was correct. I had to witness to the sanctity of life. I thanked her and asked her if she would help me write this witness.

I told Vera Marie that I wanted to donate the proceeds from this book and any other associated events relating to my witness to her nonprofit to witness to the sanctity of life.

Albert
Lifschultz

Albert with Vera Marie Verna
discussing the editing of
Warrior's Witness.

Chapter 16

Marriage to My Dear Wife Midge

I began dictating my biography. Vera Marie was busy with the architects to finish the proposed assisted living and then continue with the design for the 14-bed maternity house and child care center, for infants to age five, that would house 80 children. I visited the proposed site with my wheel chair and custom car. I prayed with her there at the proposed site in Boca Raton. She mentioned that she had owned a restaurant and also had experience with design and she was now working on the two kitchens for the assisted living.

I commented to her that she meant the main kitchen? She said no. Two fully-equipped kitchens. One would be a kosher kitchen with food to be blessed by a rabbi. She said she planned this facility to be non-denominational as the bishop of Palm Beach County had told her to make it nondenominational. She knew there was a need in the area for true kosher. She also had included in the plans her request for three chapels, one Catholic, Jewish, and non-denominational.

I told Vera Marie that I would help her with the design for the kosher kitchen and the main kitchen as I had worked at the Pentagon as a food advisor for the military, and that my parents had owned a renowned kosher catering business in New Jersey. She was so grateful for the assistance. We continued with the dictation and tape recordings.

My wife died in the nursing home, and I became unable to move due to old injuries. I had to have a bar installed over my bed so that I could pull myself up and the nurse would assist me to an upright position.

This routine went on for about a year as I continued with the dictation of the biography. Vera Marie would find an hour here and there and drive over to help with the book. I also continued to advise her about the setup for the kitchens and which equipment, etc., would be most beneficial.

After about a year, I was no longer able to drive and was pretty much bedridden, but my days were peaceful, and I accepted my condition, managing alone at my villa home with the day nurse and depending on a kind, Christian neighbor and his family to help me in the evenings.

In the mornings, the nurse would arrive. The Veterans hospital tried all kinds of therapy, but it wasn't working. My old eye injuries were catching up with me too. I began to lose my eyesight from the shrapnel wounds. The shrapnel was still imbedded under my eyes. The shots helped for a while, but eventually were less effective.

I was surprised when my former acquaintance and dear friend Midge, who lost her husband as well, said yes when I asked her to marry me. I could not believe she said yes. She is younger and better looking than myself. Most of all, she is a very devoted Christian woman. I gave my prayers of gratitude to the Father for her. Midge owned a property in Fort Lauderdale and a home in Tennessee where her son and grandson lived.

We immediately married and began to spend the summers up in Tennessee and the winters at my villa in Florida. The dictation of my biography continued long distance and was slowly progressing.

Eventually, it became difficult for us to make the drive, as not even the electric wheelchair could get the job done. We had to return now permanently to my Florida villa. The physical therapy continued, but since I turned 91 years old, I am completely bedridden. I cannot sit upright and cannot read my Bible due to the old eye injuries. I do get to pray the Lord's Prayer and Psalm 23 every day. I rejoice that my God has been so faithful as He promised. I thank Him every day for my beautiful wife.

This God-fearing wife was given me like Job of the Old Testament. I have been restored.

I thank Him for restoring my life. Restored to peace beyond all understanding. I lay here and write my poems, and this one, titled "The Man I Am," so very well sums it up.

The Man I Am

I have lived my life to see the light!

Fought through the darkest night

Have been to hell on earth

Now, thanks to God, I know my worth

My Lord awakens me every day

The devil and his followers are kept away

Because of God's most perfect plan

My trials have made me the man I am.

Midge and Albert Lifschultz

OBITUARY

Albert Irwin Lifschultz

JANUARY 8, 1928 – JULY 2, 2018

Lifschultz, Albert I CW4, US Army retired, born 8 January 1927 to Gustave and Rose Lifschultz in Irvington, NJ. Graduated Central High School, Newark, NJ and Pratt School of Business, NYC with a degree in Business Administration.

Grew up working in the family business, Clinton Manor Caterers, Clinton, NJ and Terrace Garden Hotel in Hunter, NY.

Served in the US Army through three wars – WWII, Korea, and Vietnam going from Private to Chief Warrant Officer 4 and still had time for a stage career in musical comedies and racing sports cars as an owner-driver for NASCAR.

He was an owner of Barnes Auto Parts in Irvington, NJ and 1001 Auto Parts, Woodbridge, NJ and East Brunswick, NJ.

Mr. Lifschultz was married to Mimi Benzell (deceased), Zara Kotner (deceased), and Renee Lightman for 42 years (deceased). He is survived by his current wife, Mildred Roth Lifschultz, a daughter and three grandchildren and great grandchildren.

Poetry by Albert Lifschultz

ᕔ

Rosegale
12/19/1965–3/30/1970

A little girl who nestled in our arms

Now in the Lord's protection from harm

A smiling face and a heart of gold

We staved and felt her hands grow cold

With all the prayers a family could give

She tried with every breath she said

God wants us to forgive

Left behind a grieving dying mother alone

And a father to grieve and roam

Now with the passing of many years

Finally with yours and God's help

Forgiveness is mine without tears.

~November 12, 2010

Our God Is Great

Our God is good, our God is great

He stands beside us day or night

Though we hurt Him in so many ways

He never leaves, He always stays

Slow to anger, fast to forgive

His only Son for us He did give

Our God is so good

Our God is so great.

~January 8, 2010

A Job Well Done

I have seen the dawning of another day

Left my home to see the neighbors'
  children play

All is right with my Lord and me.

My life without all turmoil peaceful as
  can be

A caring wife to take care of my many
  needs

A life now without the world's greeds

A holiday spent with friends and
  comrades in arms

Talking of memories of years in the past

As 60 years of service go by so fast.

Will there be a gun salute and taps for
  me

An 87-year-old forgotten tree.

As I sit waiting next to my Lord's left
  knee

To greet friends and relatives from long
  ago

His words, "Chief Lifschultz, a job well
  done."

~December 28, 2013

The Man I Am

I have lived my life to see the light!

Fought through the darkest night

Have been to hell on earth

Now, thanks to God, I know my worth

My Lord awakens me every day

The devil and his followers are kept away

Because of God's most perfect plan

My trials have made me the man I am.

Old Soldier's Dream

The terror and dreams that come with
  the night

Have all disappeared completely from
  sight

No bad dreams or terror to recall

Only the peace that comes from reading
  Peter and Paul

The comfort you feel when you have no
  wars to fight

Allows me now to sleep through the
  night

Now thanks to God I can try and forget
  all I left behind

Dear Lord Jesus, thank you for the
  protection and for calming my fears

When I was about to lose my (nerve)
  mind.

~March 2, 2014

Haiti

An earthquake came to a neighboring land

Destroying all the work of God's helping hand

To sinner and saint the pain not restricted

Rich and dirt poor equally inflicted

All the nations in the world

Responded with assets untold

United States sent survival equipment

And our angels to risk their lives

An angel carried

Decaying humanity's ruins and rubble

Their every little movement risk double.

But our angels' feelings soar to a new glory

When searching what once was a home
  with furniture and toys

Alive and crying an angel called out.

I just found a baby boy.

~November 22, 2010

Happy Baby Puppy Beagle,
Lifschultz the First

A baby puppy came home to stay

He would jump all over me to play

A heart full of love right from the start

Long before we knew he was very
  smart

Uncle Joe would have to go for a walk
  with his hello

Any other relative got an embarrassing
  sniff below

He saved the best for my wife

The lady whose protection he swore for
  life

At exactly five o'clock on the dot

To the front door he was Johnny-on-
  the-spot

A leap, a kiss on the face, then carried
  to my chair

Happy, at age 15, we still called puppy

Loved us equal he always played fair.

~November 19, 2010

Beau

The charm and grace of a woman's
  grace

Like the moon and the stars shining
  from above

True love more precious even than gold

With God's blessing never grows cold

Though time and tide may keep you
  apart

Those beautiful memories will live in
  your heart

When all your worldly goods start to
  crumble

It is her sense of humor and laugh that
  make your fears tumble

The magic of her warm embrace and
  kiss

Will always be the thing you will miss

No matter where you have to go

Deep in your heart you will know

No matter what or why, you are her beau.

~February 10, 2010

A Poem for Mother

Call her mother—call her mom

She's that special lady your dad calls
  wife.

But she's the lady who will guide your
  way through life

She'll dry your eyes when you've had a
  fight with the boyfriend of the week,

And she'll rub your tummy when you
  are sick and feel weak.

She's that gentle person who stood
  beside you when you married,

Who loved all the children that you
  later carried.

She's the person you will always miss
  whenever things go wrong

That woman who tagged along all her
  life.

~March 25, 2017

About the Editor

Vera Marie Verna is the director of Holy Family House, Inc., a nonprofit which serves intergenerational residents, from the elderly to young mothers-to-be. Vera Marie is also the proud mother of three adopted children. She resides in Boca Raton, Florida.

For more information about the intergenerational care centers that can be built in your area, please contact Vera Marie by email at vmvpraisejesus@gmail.com.

Holy Family House

Intergenerational Care Centers

About Leonine Publishers

Leonine Publishers LLC makes fine Catholic literature available to Catholics throughout the English-speaking world. Leonine Publishers offers an innovative "hybrid" approach to book publication that helps authors as well as readers. Please visit our web site at www.leoninepublishers.com to learn more about us. Browse our online bookstore to find more solid Catholic titles to uplift, challenge, and inspire.

Our patron and namesake is Pope Leo XIII, a prudent, yet uncompromising pope during the stormy years at the close of the 19th century. Please join us as we ask his intercession for our family of readers and authors.

www.leoninepublishers.com